Sophia's Gift

May 2024
Dollology luncheon
event

There were always
dolls ~

Karen B. Kurtz

Gratitude to *Antique DOLL Collector* and *Civil War Times* where Karen's work appeared in slightly different form and under other titles. Karen B. Kurtz acknowledges support and recognition from the 2010 Coleman Award for Research in Antique Dolls, United Federation of Doll Clubs, Kansas City, Missouri; 2014 Seven Hills Literary Contest, Tallahassee, Florida; 2015 Writers-Editors Network International Writing Competition, North Stratford, New Hampshire; and Pensters Writing Group, Fairhope, Alabama.

Thanks go to Elizabeth Ann Coleman; Janet Gula; Linda Edward; Loretta Nardone; curator Cathy Wright, Edinburgh, Scotland; curator Robert Hancock at American Civil War Museum, Richmond, Virginia; librarian Julie Bushong, Culpeper County Library, Culpeper, Virginia; researcher Grace Zell, Beth Ahabah Museum and Archives, Richmond, Virginia; Grace Darling Museum, Bamburgh, UK; Dr. Adam Prince, Adele Stafford, Dr. Philip Levin, Rabbi Steven Silberman, and Cheryl Glicker.

Historical Note credits go to American Civil War Museum for images of the doll Grace Darling; The Photolibrary Wales /Alamy Stock Photo for Grace Horsley Darling rowing the boat; Culpeper County Library and Library of Congress, Geography and Map Division, 1863, for maps; and Mark A. Kurtz for the author and illustrator photos.

ISBN: 978-1-945190-97-1

Intellect Publishing, LLC
Point Clear, Alabama
www.IntellectPublishing.com

Provenance

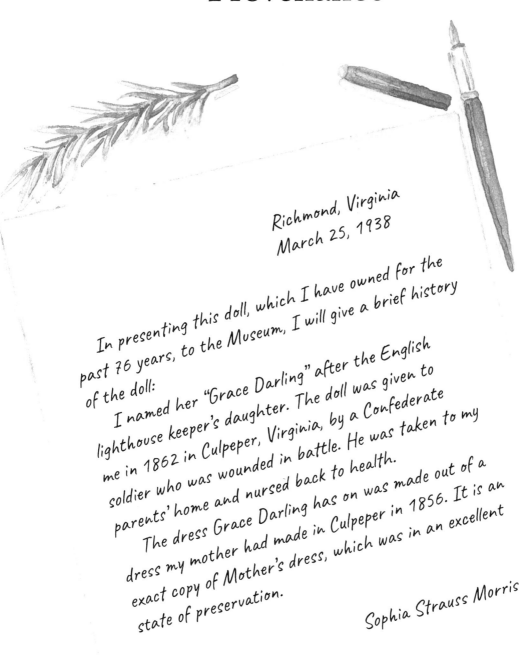

Richmond, Virginia
March 25, 1938

In presenting this doll, which I have owned for the past 76 years, to the Museum, I will give a brief history of the doll:

I named her "Grace Darling" after the English lighthouse keeper's daughter. The doll was given to me in 1862 in Culpeper, Virginia, by a Confederate soldier who was wounded in battle. He was taken to my parents' home and nursed back to health.

The dress Grace Darling has on was made out of a dress my mother had made in Culpeper in 1856. It is an exact copy of Mother's dress, which was in an excellent state of preservation.

Sophia Strauss Morris

Amid the rubble of the American Civil War, a mysterious box found its way to Culpeper, Virginia, where Sophia Strauss lived.

In their shop, Mama lifted a big china doll from the box.

"Oh, Mama, she's beautiful! I'd call her Grace Darling if she were mine!"

Mama smiled at Sophia.

"Yes, you love that old story. Time to light our *Shabbos* candle," she said, as they walked upstairs to their home.

Sophia ran to do as Mama asked.

Everyone in town scurried to help.

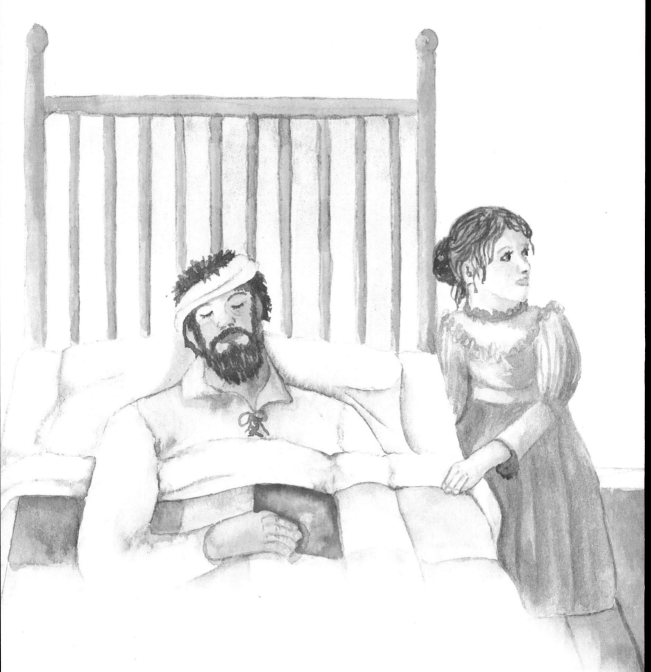

Soon, strangers carried a soldier into Sophia's bedroom. He clung to life by a thread, burning with fever. No one knew his name or rank.

"Sophia! Bring bandages! Warm water! *Schnell! Schnell!*"

Sophia applied salve to his cracked lips and cheeks.

She looked silently to
the doll for strength.

After six days, the soldier opened his eyes.

The next day thundering hooves beat out a sharp staccato on Coleman Street as Confederate cavalry galloped by.

"The Union asked for a truce to carry the wounded from battle! Trainloads of men are coming! Help us!" shouted the riders.

"Sophia, carry fragile things from the shop to your bedroom!" Mama demanded.

They were in great need of money. Sophia knew that doll was not hers, could never be hers, but secretly named it Grace Darling in her heart.

"I miss Papa."

"Yes, I hope he returns from the war soon."

Each day he grew stronger. Sophia wrote down her favorite Yiddish word and gave it to him. He told her the whole *megillah* about his family. They *kibitzed* over checkers.

When the soldier was well enough to travel, he wanted to give Sophia a token of remembrance. He opened a secret compartment in his boot, revealing a clutch of coins.

He paid Mama more than Grace Darling cost.

"I think you need this doll, Sophia. You two are very similar."

"Oh, thank you!" squealed Sophia. "I love Grace Darling so much!"

"You helped me pass the time. We all love attention when we're sick."

Time slowed after the soldier left.
Mama knitted socks for the soldiers.
Sophia rolled bandages.

They prayed to
God for better days.

Hardships increased as the war continued. More and more people left town. Prices soared. Sophia and Mama mixed ground eggshells in cornmeal. They could not waste any morsel of food.

"Would they have to sell Grace Darling for food?" Sophia worried.

Sophia loved Grace Darling deeply. She distracted Mama.
"Can we make Grace Darling a new dress?"

Mama found an old party gown in the attic. The iridescent silk
taffeta still shone. She ripped it apart. Wallpaper scraps made new
pattern pieces. Thorns held the patterns and fabric together. Mama
cut out everything and sewed Grace Darling's dress by hand. Sophia
tacked the lace with tiny stitches.

After the gown was finished, Mama and Sophia joined hands, *tanzing, tanzing, tanzing* around the room. Their skirts blew out like bells as they twirled in wide circles.

For a moment, war was forgotten.
The whole room seemed to smile.

Historical Note

Grace Darling

High in the mountains near Stutzhaus, Germany, workers at the Alt, Beck and Gottschalck factory brought Grace Darling to life from wet clay. She stood 28 inches tall. They shipped her to America in a box alongside dozens of other dolls. George Borgfeldt in New York  City bought the dolls and resold them throughout America. German dollmakers sold mountains of dolls around the world in the 1850s.

Grace Horsley Darling

Grace Horsley Darling lived in a lighthouse on the Farne Islands, off the coast of Northumberland, England. In 1838, while keeping watch, she saw the steamship *Forfarshire* run into a storm and break apart on the jagged rocks. Grace and her father, William, rowed out to help. Their task seemed impossible, but they miraculously saved nine people from sure death.

Queen Victoria recognized Grace's bravery. Poems, songs, and books about her were very popular. Grace's fame spread to America. For years afterward, mere mention of Grace Darling's name stirred people's imaginations, just as Sophia was inspired to name her doll after the famous British icon.

Sophia's Family

Sophia and her parents, Leopold and Caroline Strauss, were Jewish Confederates who lived through the American Civil War.

After the German Revolution in 1848, Leopold, who was only 18 years old, fled his homeland for a better life in America.

He met Caroline Lowenthal's father in Baltimore. Mr. Lowenthal gave Leopold a horse and wagon full of goods, which he sold to farm wives in Virginia.

Leopold bought a shop in Culpeper and married Caroline in 1856. They were the first Jews to live in this small frontier town.

Then Sophia was born.

But the Civil War destroyed their happiness. Union soldiers ransacked Leopold's shop and hauled him off to a Washington prison, where he endured wretched conditions. Leopold returned to Culpeper after the war and managed to hang onto his shop during Reconstruction's hard times.

The Strauss family grew. They were part of the guiding force that lifted Culpeper from war's rubble.

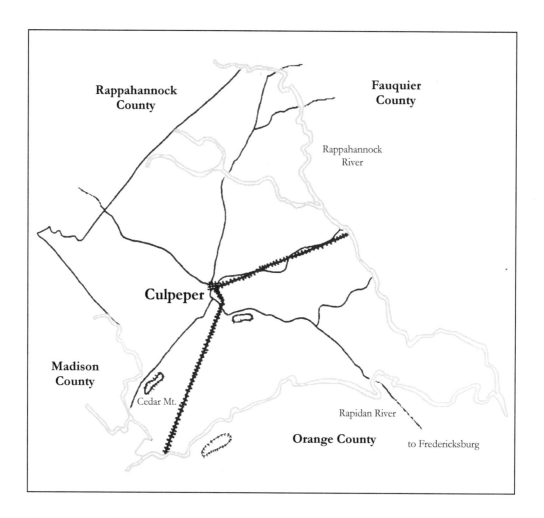

Culpeper, Virginia

Geography and circumstance made Culpeper a vortex during the American Civil War. A prized military position for both sides, Culpeper's two railroads moved supplies and troops. The Rappahannock River, and its largest tributary, the Rapidan, were easy to cross most of the year. Troops were always on the move.

More than 160 battles raged around Culpeper. The Battle of Cedar Mountain clashed eight miles from Sophia's home in August 1862. It is thought the Confederate soldier was wounded in this four-day battle, but his identity remains a mystery to this very day.

Culpeper citizens lost everything they had. Time's passage restored the land to its beauty, but even now, the magnitude of such death and destruction seems impossible to understand.

Priceless Treasure

Everyone is gone now—except the doll Grace Darling. She lives at the American Civil War Museum (www.ACWM.org) in Richmond, Virginia, a place heavy with history. Grace Darling's facial features are as bright as the day she was manufactured in Germany. Her original gown still looks fabulous.

Grace Darling's true story of courage, compassion, and perseverance is eternal, and will survive any War.

A doll is a witness
who cannot die,
with a doll
you are never alone.
—Margaret Atwood

There's rosemary, that's for remembrance.

Award-winning author **Karen B. Kurtz** has published books, essays, poetry, and countless articles for readers of all ages. *Garland of Joy: A Treasury of Dolls* is forthcoming with her husband-photographer, Mark A. Kurtz. They founded The Kurtz Kollection™, the premier line of greeting cards and stationery featuring the images of precious dolls, which sold to collectors and shops around the world. Learn more about The Kurtz Team at www.karenbkurtz.com.

Loran Chavez is an award-winning artist whose work is represented in galleries. Her art is in collections all over the world. Loran competes in multiple outdoor juried art competitions each year, completes commissions, and teaches children a love of art and recycled art forms. Follow her at www.loranchavez. blogspot.com and www.loranchavez.com.

Karen and Loran are neighbors in the community of Fairhope, Alabama, on the Eastern Shore of Mobile Bay.

CPSIA information can be obtained
at www.ICGtesting.com
Printed in the USA
BVHW060840041121
620395BV00002B/41